HOUSE OF LORDS AND COMMONS

ISHION HUTCHINSON

HOUSE OF LORDS AND COMMONS

FARRAR STRAUS GIROUX / NEW YORK

Farrar, Straus and Giroux

18 West 18th Street, New York 10011

Copyright © 2016 by Ishion Hutchinson
Printed in the United States of America

First edition, 2016

Library of Congress Cataloging-in-Publication Data

Names: Hutchinson, Ishion, author.

Title: House of lords and commons : poems / Ishion Hutchinson.

Description: First edition. | New York : Farrar, Straus and Giroux, 2016.

Identifiers: LCCN 2015045801 | ISBN 9780374173029 (hardcover) |

ISBN 9780374714543 (ebook)

Subjects: | BISAC: POETRY / American / General. | POETRY / Caribbean &

Latin American. | POETRY / American / African American.

Classification: LCC PR9265.9.H85 A6 2016 | DDC 811/.6—dc23

LC record available at http://lccn.loc.gov/2015045801

Designed by Quemadura

Our books may be purchased in bulk for promotional, educational, or
business use. Please contact your local bookseller or the Macmillan Corporate
and Premium Sales Department at 1-800-221-7945, extension 5442,
or by e-mail at MacmillanSpecialMarkets@macmillan.com.

www.fsgbooks.com

www.twitter.com/fsgbooks

www.facebook.com/fsgbooks

1 3 5 7 9 10 8 6 4 2

VALZHYNA

KORAH

TO WAYNE CHEN

Praise the barbarians invading your sleep
Their exploding horses hurting the snow

CONTENTS

HOUSE OF LORDS AND COMMONS

STATION

The train station is a cemetery.
Drunk with spirits, a man enters. I fan gnats
from my eyes to see into his face. "Father!"
I shout and stumble. He does not budge.
After thirteen years, neither snow nor train,
only a few letters, and twice, from a cell,
his hoarfrost accent crossed the Atlantic.
His mask slips a moment as in childhood,
pure departure, a gesture of smoke.

Along freighted crowds the city punished,
picking faces in the thick nest of morning's
hard light that struck raw and stupid,
searching, and in the dribble of night commuters,
I have never found him, wandering the almond
trees' shadows, since a virus disheartened
the palms' blossoms and mother gave me the sheaves
in her purse so he would remember her
and then shaved her head to a nut.

I talk fast of her in one of my Cerberus
voices, but he laughs, shaking the scales

of froth on his coat. The station's cold
cracks a hysterical congregation;
his eyes flash little obelisks that chase the spirits
out, and, without them, wavering, I see
nothing like me. Stranger, father, cackling
rat, who am I transfixed at the bottom
of the station? Pure echo in the train's
beam arriving on its cold nerve of iron.

FITZY AND THE
REVOLUTION

The rumour broke first in Duckenfield.
Fitzy dropped the shutters of his rum shop.
By the time it got to Dalvey there were three suicides.
The mechanic in Cheswick heard and gave his woman
a fine trashing; but, to her credit, she nearly scratched his heart
out his chest during the howl and leather smithing.

The betting shops and the whorehouse Daylights
at Golden Grove were empty; it was brutal
to see the women with their hands at their jaws on the terrace;
seeing them you know the rumour was not rumour,
the rumour was gospel: the cane cutters did not get their salary.

Better to crucify Christ again.
Slaughter newborns, strike down the cattle,
but to make a man not have money in his pocket on a payday
Friday was abomination itself; worse cane cutters,
who filed their spines against the sun, bringing down great walls
    of cane.

You'd shudder to see them, barebacked men, bent kissing
the earth, so to slash away the roots of the canes;
every year the same men, different cane, and when different
    men,
the same cane: the cane they cannot kill, living for this one day

of respite when they'd straighten themselves to pillars
and drop dollars on counters and act like Daylights is a suite
at the Ritz and the devastating beauty queens with their gaulin
fragile attention gave them forever to live in a tickle, the whetted
canepiece, this one day, forgotten in a whore's laugh.

Suddenly these men filled Hampton Court square
demanding the foreman's head.
They were thirsty for blood and for rum.
Fitzy stayed hidden in his shop behind the shutters.
He heard one man say it was not the foreman's head they
    should get,
that would not be wise.
The man continued: it must be fire for fire;
the factory must be burnt down.

But the men murmured. They were afraid.
Someone made a joke, they roared,
and soon they were saying fire can't buy rum,

they were roaring money, then rum, pounding Fitzy's shutter,

shouting his name for him to set them on fire.

They grew hoarse against the shutters.

The sun had taken all motion out of their voices.

Fitzy could hear them through the zinc,

like dogs about to die, cried-out children, that dry rustle

you hear after the crop is torched and the wind bristles the
    ashes.

No men were out there. Only a shirring noise.

That was when Fitzy opened the shutters.

Their red eyes in charcoal suits looked up at him,

and with an overseer's scorn, he nodded them in.

INFERNO

FOR J. MAXWELL, JOURNALIST

Standing in this motorcade of rusting
ideas, you sighed: *non serviam.* What for?
If they can jail the sea, draw borders
with their San San, Grand Lido and Hilton,
what would they do to your cumulus head
and the wobbling knots you go around on?

Everything ripens in the road—
a mouth shines the mic, pomade-melting
words, a dark-glassed savant imploding
through his tight collar, words, words, yes!
a flurry of bell beats; they hammer rings
of pot covers and lift scarlet banners
towards the sky; electric wires stretch
three vicious scrawls into the day.

You turn, old man, from the crowd,
deep in its frenzied coal pot, visibly
shaken when speakers command the trucks,

and they rumble forward, legions,
a spectral army, or animals, despoiled
of reason.

       You will not serve, not here,
not even among the quiet asphodels.

BICYCLE ECLOGUE

That red bicycle left in an alley near the Ponte Vecchio,
I claim; I claim its elongated shadow, ship crested on
stacked crates; I claim the sour-mouth Arno and the stone
arch bending sunlight on vanished medieval fairs;
but mostly I claim this two-wheel chariot vetching
on the wall, its sickle fenders reaping dust and pollen
off the heat-congested city coiled to a halt in traffic.
And I, without enough for the great museums,
am struck by the red on the weathered brick, new tyres
on cobble, the bronze tulip bell—smaller than Venus's nose—
turned up against the river, completely itself for itself.
The scar in my palm throbs, recalling a tiny stone
once stuck there after I fell off the district's iron mule,
welded by the local artisan, Barrel Mouth—no relation
of Botticelli—the summer of my first long pants.
The doctor's scissors probing my flesh didn't hurt,
nor the lifeline bust open when the stone was plucked out;
what I wailed for that afternoon was the anger in mother's
face when she found out I had disobeyed her simple wish
to remain indoors until she returned from kneeling
in the harvested cane, tearing out the charred roots

from the earth after cane cutters had slashed the burnt field.
It was her first day, and her last, bowing so low to pull
enough for my school fee; for, again, the promised money
didn't fall from my father's cold heaven in England.
As we walked to the clinic on a rabble of hogplums,
her mouth trembled in her soot frock, my palm reddened
in her grip, plum scent taking us through the lane.
By the time we saw the hospital's rusty gate, her fist
was stained to my fingers' curl, and when I unfastened
my eyes from the ground to her face, gazing ahead, terribly calm
in the hail of sunlight, a yellow shawl around her head,
something of shame became clear, and if I had more
sense as my blood darkened to sorrel at the age
of twelve or thirteen, I would have forgotten the sting
and wreathed tighter my hold before letting her go.
And now, as I raise my camera, bells charge the pigeon
sky braced by the Duomo, a shell fallen from the sun.
I kneel, snap the cycle, rise, hurry away.

PUNISHMENT

All the dead eyes of the dead
on portraits behind her looked
down as she ate donuts off
a cloth napkin, her mouth
sugared. I saw myself possessed
by myself in her glasses' milky
lens that possessed the globe
on her desk, a Quaker gift the former
principal, dead but not yet
a portrait, left with Africa
spun towards us. She swallowed,
then asked why was I here.
I told her, for intimations.

She stopped mid-chew, surplice
of sugar danced at the down
curl of her lips. She said *Excuse me*.
I continued: for immortality.

She looked with cow-out-of-pasture
concern, the others' eyes scalded
through me, the clock fell

silent though the second hand
wheeled around the white face.
For my freshness, she said,
You must be punished:
you must go out to the cemetery
by the chapel, write down
every last living name off
the tombstones before she arrived.

No problem, I knew the dead.
I was well off with their names.
But, she asked, a fresh donut
christened the napkin, if I am clear
why she has done this,
why she must punish me.

The portraits drew one breath.
I began: for my rejection
of things past,
because, for my life, the green graves
by the chapel puzzle me
and the sea outside our classroom,
those ships no one else sees,
humming, humming
their frail sails, join us,
though I don't know who us is.

She rose, utterly black;

I retreated, she filed

past the cabinet,

upset the globe;

I whirled out

the door; there

cliffs and clouds,

the dark manchineel

blinding the path

I bolted down,

hardly believing

my legs running

and leaping

above ground,

straight down

Hector's River

sea-road, flanked

by the hushed,

breaking sea.

AFTER THE HURRICANE

After the hurricane walks a silence, deranged, white as the
    white helmets
of government surveyors looking into roofless

shacks, accessing stunned fowls, noting inquiries
into the logic of feathers, reversed, like gullies still retching;
    they scribble facts

about fallen cedars, spread out like dead generals on leaf
medallions; they draw tables to show the shore

has rearranged its idea of beauty for the resort
villas, miraculously not rattled by the hurricane's—

call it Cyclops—passage through the lives
of children and pigs, the one eye that unhooked

banjos from the hills, smashed them in Rio Valley;
they record how it howled off to that dark parish

St. Thomas, stomping drunk with wire lashes and cramps,
paralyzing electric poles and coconut trees,

dishing discord among neighbours, exposed,
standing among their flattened, scattered lives for the first time.

It passed through Aunt May's head, upsetting
the furniture, left her chattering something,

a cross between a fowl and a child; they can't say
how it tore down her senses, no words, packing

their instruments, flies returning to genuflect
at their knees, on Aunt May's face, gone soft;

no words, except: *Don't fret*, driving off,
as if they had left better promises to come.

A MARCH

Lesson of the day: Syria and Styria.
For Syria, read: *His conquering banner shook from Syria.*
And for Styria: Look at this harp of blood, mapping.

Now I am tuned. I am going to go above
my voice for the sake of the forest shaken
on the bitumen. You can see stars in the skulls,

winking, synapses, intermittent, on edge
of shriek—perhaps a cluster of fir, birches?—
Anyway. Don't get too hung up

on the terms; they have entropy
in common, bad for the public weal,
those obtuse centurions in the flare

of the bougainvillea, their patent-seeking
gift kindled. Divers speech. Cruelty.
Justice. Never mind, but do

pay attention to the skirmish—the white
panther that flitters up the pole—
its shade grows large on the ground.

THE GARDEN

The streetlights shed pearls that night,
stray dogs ran but did not bark at the strange
shadows; the Minister of All could not sleep,
mosquitoes swarmed around his net,
his portrait and his pitcher and drinking glass;
the flags stiffened on the embassy building but
did not fall when the machine guns
flared and reminded that stars were inside
the decrepit towns, in shanty-zinc holes,
staring at the fixed constellation; another
asthmatic whirl of pistons passed,
the chandelier fell, the carpet sparkled,
flames burst into the lantana bushes, the stone
horse whinnied by the bank's marble entrance,
three large cranes with searchlights lit
the poincianas, a quiet flamboyance, struck
with the fever of children's laughter;
then, all at once, the cabbage palms
and the bull-hoof trees shut their fans,
the harbour grew empty and heavy,
the sea was sick and exhausted, the royal

palms did not salute when the jeeps roamed

up the driveway and circled the fountain,

the blue mahoe did not bow and the lignum

vitae shed purple bugles but did not

surrender, the homeless did not run, but the dead

flew in a silver stream that night, their silk

hair thundered and their heels crushed

the bissy nuts and ceramic roofs;

the night had the scent of cut grass

sprayed with poison, the night smelled

of bullets, the moon did not hide,

the prisoners prayed in their bunkers,

the baby drank milk while its mother slept,

and by the window its father

could not part the curtains.

THE DIFFERENCE

They talk oil in heavy jackets and plaid over
their coffee, they talk Texas and the north cold,

but mostly oil and Obama, voices dipping
vexed and then they talk Egypt failing,

Greek broken and it takes cash for France not
charity and I rather speak Russia than Ukraine

one says in rubles, than whatever, whatever
the trouble, because there is sea and gold,

a tunnel, wherever right now, an-anyhow-Belarus,
oh, I will show you something, conspiring

coins, this one, China, and they marvel,
their minds hatched crosses, a frontier

zeroed not by voyage or pipeline nor the milk
foam of God, no, not the gutsy weather they talk

frizzled, the abomination worsening
opulence to squalor, never the inverse.

A FARTHER SHORE

1

By the shadowless lion-bluff of Pigeon
Island, you have gone swimming, a clear
afternoon, children's faint play noises ring
in the yard by the hyphened church school near
century-old cafés, one with a zinc fence signed in comic
icons: ICE CREAM AND OTHER SUPPLIES,
scythes your sides with laughter, but they vanish
near the beach stretch, the piratical hoteliers'
paradise, a white army of luxury boats idled,
processional, waiting for a flare to blow
and ignite another plantation, without Bible
or chain, just the PM's handshake and bow.
You ignore them for your first immersion.
The blue water whitens and collects you in its salt mine.

2

Aw, *viejo*, so this is the chessboard you wrote

about, as by sleight, an emerald, patient army

poised for your command, a voice without

force to crack the terra-cotta quiet, steadily

erect between two flailing lives; memory

and this, the present, advancing only down,

the body's tower rattled by what it carries:

diabetes and your gift, the mighty, unscathed morne.

We will not mourn at the bishop's speech

that day, not when he crosses himself twice, an X;

we will be like the breakers on the beach

at Cas-en-Bas, mute with rage, serenely vexed

that your life is not a chess game, played again

in the shade, with other shades, companions

literature, not language, has made aware

of the others' ignorance, shifting in time.

HOMAGE: VALLEJO

Brailed up from birth, these obdurate, obituary corners
of second life the hospital light–ravened solstice

blessed with a caesarean and now we have a republic,
the bread-under-arm water bearer of the sea: Cetus, Christ.

After the blackbird I put on my herringbone jacket,
the feather-hummed gargoyles bearing down buildings,

rain scowled down, *Vallejo* and *Vallejo* as I hurried
up Eager Street; Thursday, I remember the white stone

in the flask and wild asterisks hissing; Thursdays, falling
at noon, at Cathedral Street, blackbirds falling quietly at
    Biddle Street.

THE ARK BY "SCRATCH"

The genie says build a studio. I build
a studio from ash. I make it out of peril and slum
things. I alone when blood and bullet and all
Christ-fucking-'Merican-dollar politicians talk
the pressure down to nothing, when the equator's
confused and coke bubbles on tinfoil to cemented wreath.
I build it, a Congo drum, so hollowed through the future
pyramids up long before CDs spin away roots-men knocking
    down by the seaside,
like captives wheeling by the Kebar River. The genie says build
a studio, but don't take any fowl in it, just electric.
So I make it, my echo chamber with shock rooms of rainbow
King Arthur's sword keep in, and one for the Maccabees
alone, for covenant is bond between man and worm.
Next room is Stone Age, after that, Iron, and one I
named Freeze, for too much ice downtown in the brains
of all them crossing Duke Street, holy like parsons.
And in the circuit breaker, the red switch is for death
and the black switch is for death, and the master switch
is black and red, so if US, Russia, China, Israel talk
missiles talk, I talk that switch I call Melchizedek.

I build a closet for the waterfalls. One for the rivers.
Another for oceans. Next for secrets. The genie says build
a studio. I build it without gopher wood. Now, consider
the nest of bees in the cranium of the Gong, consider
the nest of wasps in the heart of the Bush Doctor,
consider the nest of locusts in the gut of the Black Heart Man,
I put them there, and the others that vibrate at the Feast of the
    Passover when the collie weed
is passed over the roast fish and cornbread. I Upsetter, I Django
on the black wax, the Super Ape, E.T., I cleared the wave.
Again, consider the burning bush in the ears of Kalonji
and the burning sword in the mouth of the Fireman and the
    burning pillar in the eyes
of the Gargamel, I put them there, to outlast earth as I navigate
    on one
of Saturn's rings, I mitre solid shadow, setting fire to snow in
    my ark.
I credit not the genie but the coral rock: I man am stone.
I am perfect. Myself is a vanishing conch shell speeding round
a discothèque at the embassy of angels, skeletons ramble to
    check out
my creation dub and sex is dub, stripped to the bone, and dub
    is the heart
breaking the torso to spring, olive beaked, to be eaten up by
    sunlight.

PRELUDE TO THE AFTERNOON OF A FAUN

Noon ictus cooling the veranda's
fretwork, the child sits after his harp
boning burlesque in the bower, his slit
of gulls' nerves silenced into hydrangea.
Violet and roan, the bridal sun is
opening and closing a window,
filling a clay pot of coins with coins;
candle jars, a crystal globe, cut milk
boxes with horn petals snapping
their iceberg-Golgotha crackle.
The loneliness is terrible, the ice is near,
says the hasp-lipped devil, casting
beatitudes at the castor-oiled pimps
in Parliament; Pray for them, joyfully,
their amazing death! Light seethes
bulging like pipes blown with napalm
from his big golden eyes, turning
the afternoon ten degrees backwards,
then through palm fronds' teething
the bridled air, sprigs of goat hair, fall.

A BURNT SHIP

Tiger moth, hair smoke, silk tied,
her mouth's not the chamber angel,

the night chimera that comes
to the boy on the alabaster throne,

no longer child-king of Sumer,
his trigger-blood hammers rust,

strings of charm, shards of jewels
glint like sunset oil, streak shield

held closely in the singing woods
of bat-eaten fruits, silently hanging

blot seeds, cut sage and rosemary,
a blight mercury, cured meat,

silver streams dividing undersea
the ultraviolet weeds, plankton,

seahorse, half man, sunken masks,
god's horn, perfume, ivory tusks,

market dust, vine pillars, batter-ram
sound, orange-light caravan, wheels

of water spinning industry, whipped
backs, shock foil, the galvanized wax

congealed dreams of a burnt ship;
all were lost, all were drowned.

OCTOBER'S LEVANT

1

Dusk, a pair of goats clamber up the hill,
their soft cries suggesting a child where
there is none, a living creature with a spirit
in a cold cell, lying on newspapers soiled
with the burdens of unknown men, granite music
in his ears, and though he must not hope,
hope is there in the starved hole in his chest,
wrenching sunlight and memory: shadows trawl
the sand where he lies, half-asleep to the surf,
gravelly like his grandfather's throat clearing
at daybreak, before cycling down the fern
path to the tuber ground; the child shifts
to the grove of unripe sea pears no ant nest
thrives in, and he must speak his presence,
his blood-weight to this land water scrapes
away, foam reaching for his back, now a log,
brown and dry, suggesting a boy where
there is none; he stands, unrevealed, the slate
voice of return bobbing an urn in his gullet.

2

By now the pouis of Mona are in full bloom,
the plain crimson and crystal where a slave
plantation tans away in the heat's coffer,

a broke eldorado a young general once, buckling
his uniform early in the morning, looks out
his window at another mote of the Empire,

does not foresee his subjects, unburdened,
passing underneath the aqueducts near the library
and theatre, into exam rooms, poui scent furious

in their gossip cut short when the electric
bell shrieks them to attention, and they consider
"the commonwealth on an even beam,"

the invigilator's wristwatch ticks the sun
to inch a digit, then another, and another,
as a breeze snipes the flambeaux of the trees.

3

Four months after the Tivoli invasion, a new
market has opened where the old one was flattened
by fire; the garbage is elsewhere, even the ribbed
mongrels are absent, gone before the army
bulldozed the carapaces of burnt-out cars,
refrigerators and gas cylinders, to make a balm-yard
clearing, blood flowed and compounded tribal
rifts into an estuary crabbed with the dead;
and not blood alone, for there was no blood
when those stalls were scoured with lime; salt
glinted off their galvanized shutters like portals
the *Man*, the Gorgon, Don of Dons, the President-Minister-
   Chief,
leapt through either to America or to hell
(likely Hell America, FEMA; likely the Playboy Mansion),
but that was just flatulence from uptown mouths;
for in the shingled streets, behind barbed territories,
concrete walls consecrated with bullets, something
else flashed in the curfewed moonlight that scraped
across the exploded Shell building's blank windows,
gaping at tankers asleep like riddled sphinxes
in an oasis of splinters; a whole other story glowed:
"him still here, you know," the stars winked,
meaning, he will always be here, weighing our lives.

4

I must not be too surprised at the sudden
rain while writing to you, crisply departed,
for no matter how far I have moved from home,
this always reins me in, the sight of rain
and sunlight together, childhood's leavened joy
back-spinning us fast downhill after
stuffing ourselves with my granny's cakes
and ginger beer, and you, ever the fleet-foot
playfield king, always ahead, so far ahead
a cloud has eaten your voice and I your dust;
yes, you weigh heavily on me, friend,
who no longer knows the way to die.

5

"And there was no more sea," the Levantine
writes in his logbook, undoubtedly
stealing from the Book of Revelation.

Everything recedes like a scroll, the acacias
crick when you walk under them towards
the lonely beach, these things in my head:

"And for the soul if it is to know itself
it is into a soul that it must look" and
"the Aegean flower with corpses."

October, inconsolable, the asphalt
bordering the seagrass, warm and silver
in the blazing afternoon, so I know
I am alive and you are not. No matter

how sure I am that it is going to be there,
even after a new Heaven and a new Earth,
once I have crossed the crest by the grove

of sea pears and I sit on a log, facing it,
the white detonating curtain, the sea, our sea,
"where I left you thinking I would return," I weep.

MOVED BY THE BEAUTY OF TREES

The beauty of the trees stills her;
she is stillness staring at the leaves,

still and green and keeping up the sky;
their beauty stills her and she is quiet

in her stare, her eyes' long lashes curve
and keep, her little mouth opens

and keeps still with its quiet for the beauty
of the trees, their leaves, the sky

and its blue quiet, very still and quiet;
her looking eyes wide, deep, silent

hard on the trees and the beauty
of the sky, the green of the leaves.

PHAETON

Ground-levelled, behind a line drawn,
he took aim at a circle of precious marbles,
precise, interrupting the passing ants,
the shot was fired, and if they had known,
the other boys, that before speaking, the poet
of old had also bent and stroked the earth,
dividing himself from his people—
if they had known any poet—they would
have stopped him before the sun burst
from his fingers, scattering glass beads.

They found him with an empty third eye
the bullet drilled into his forehead, a deaf
hole, knowing only its own darkness there
in the parched-grass field; flies whirred
a sun-chariot's axle-songs; heat rose a mirror
before his skull, and his mouth opened,
amazed to this mask, its bleached stillness,
like a stone lit from the inside, faded,
a moon marked in the dust—at this face,
his mouth opened, amazed, stayed opened.

PIERRE

It was a boy named Pierre Powell
who was in charge of the atlas

in the cabinet. He also ended days
by shaking the iron bell from Principal

William's window, a work we grudged
him for very little; what cut our cores

twice a week and we had to endure,
was him being summoned to fetch

the key, again from William's office,
to open the varnished box with the world

map, old and laminated, a forbidden
missionary gift trophied beside the Oxford

Set of Mathematical Instruments and other
things seen only by Pierre and teacher Rose,

who now only nodded to raise him
to his duty. We waited in quiet

his return, Miss Rose all crinkled blouse
and bones with chalk dust in her hair,

did not stir until he was back, panting
at the door. Another diviner's nod

and he opened it, unrolled the map expertly,
kneaded out creases and held down edges

for the ruler our eyes followed,
screeching out countries, and etched

in the periphery, a khaki-pillared Pierre,
with a merchant's smile, a fixed blur

in our cry of Algeria, Switzerland, Chile,
soon withered away, and we eyed the field

of dry grass outside, a rusty mule,
statue-frozen in the punishable heat,

Pierre, a phantom sea fraying
over Antarctica, Fiji, Belize, India

of those still in the rote, a liturgy of dunce
bats, whose one cardinal point, Tropicana

Sugar Estate, so close we could smell the sugar
being processed, whistled its shift change,

and terminated Geography. As if punched
from dream, those of us gazers spared the map-

rolling-up and cabinet-locking ceremony,
saw him, with a cord-strung key, an earnest air

bearing him away in a portal of sunlight.
He was absent the week before summer,

and when Miss Rose, in rare fashion,
inquired, a girl said he had gone back home.

"Home," Miss Rose sounded the strange word.
"Home," the girl echoed and added, "him from Cayman,

Miss, or Canada, somewhere with a C."
We turned to Miss Rose to clarify Canada

or Cayman, this elsewhere C curdled
to snow in our minds; foreign always spectral,

but she pointed anonymously a crooked
finger and said, "Run to the principal

for the key," the whole class scattered, paid
no heed that not a single one was ordained.

SIBELIUS AND MARLEY

History is dismantled music; slant,
bleak on gravel. One amasses silence,
another chastises silence with nettles,
stinging ferns. I oscillate in their jaws.

The whole gut listens. The ear winces
white nights in his talons: sinking mire.
He wails and a comet impales the sky
with the duel wink of a wasp's burning.

Music dismantles history; the flambeaux
inflame in his eyes with a locust plague,
a rough gauze bolting up his mouth unfolds,
so he lashes the air with ropes and roots

that converge on a dreadful zero,
a Golden Age. Somewhere, an old film.
Dusk solders on a cold, barren coast. There
I am a cenotaph of horns and stones.

THE WANDERER

Still clear from its very first shout, "Thalatta! Thalatta!"
is the clamour every wave brings, 10,000 voices
arched into one, shaking the mountain clouds down

to mist, power they sing, spitting salt into flames, to outlast
the memory of those who toiled with the mongoose
and snake, never to sit like a colossal Memnon as his songs

turn into brass croaks, language reentering the guttural
cave before the first spark of flint. I can tell you this, boy,
history is that rusty anchor holding no ship in the bay;

it's mineral, natural as colonies of polyps in the reef.
I am no paragon of science; I am a drifter, a sea swift
some poet once used to make a crest in Time. Thunder

rifts the grain of his epochs, spinning Cortés from quartz,
repeating Pizarro along with all the names that depopulated
the trees of parrots and stuck a yellow disease in the sand.

There the steel fronds of unsheathed Christianity speared
the souls of the arrowroot and wild maize and erected bells
rid the clanging shells of their healing.

          The chattering beads

went silent, the porous rocks choked in the ceremonial basin,

the earth absorbed the goat's blood (same blood that gave
          the soil

around these parts its colour). You cannot trust the sea.

But it's good to arrive in such a peaceful harbour. How lucky

you are to sit ignorant of which Caesar roams this century.

All our heroes are asleep in that aqua-grave, they will not drift

like Xenophon's army to shore, and change their cry

to Triana's "Tierra! Tierra!" Light; land: substance.

          Both cries have congealed

into one coral wreath in my ears. I hear them everywhere I go.

MARKING IN VENICE

I hop off the vaporetto mooring in
the after-storm harbour, puff-chested, shouting:
"Keep up your bright swords, for the dew will rust them,"

hitting over a handkerchief vendor—allusions
are cheap on Piazza San Marco—Desdemonas
everywhere, clutching skirts wilding the wind.

My first time, yet a return (islands have that trick
about them; Jamaica, Cyprus). I roam alleys Iago's
betrayal rivals the pigeons' shit; soccer fans

block the opera doors, dart in and out of bars,
their cheers rise, an ensemble of drunk violins;
even now, now, very now, a waiter crashes

his shield tray in the horde and is swallowed
by the hydra. But I stray from the Basilica's
hard gleam, the afternoon coagulates and shows

a pale sign above an arch: GHETTO VECCHIO,
and I see an old man and a girl, Gottlieb's subjects,
walking to, or from, synagogue, the shadow

of enlightenment encroaches and dogs them:
"Be a Jew at home, and a man outside."
Their exile infects and reminds me this is no

vacation, just hate's old transfiguration, language's
treason, the savage cause carved in stone.
A lamp blows out in his beard, gravels of nimbus

reconvene; God grumbles in his mirrored palace,
for he knows he has loved wisely but not well.

GIRL AT CHRISTMAS

For all she's gladdened: milk
dreaming love in one hand;
clefts of clementine stain

the other. They cannot die;
the coral joy and battering
ceramic, the peach bones

and scotch bonnet seeds;
the sorrel, and foil mask she then puts
on to belt her savage choir.

THE LORDS AND COMMONS OF SUMMER

1

I circled half-mad a dead azalea scent that framed
my room; I licked anointed oil off a sardine tin,

opened *Being and Time*, perplexed myself, then picked up
and blew a clay bird whistle, silence came scratching,

the same way it did at the funeral of Heidegger,
when no silence came.

2

When my boy-self played séance in the Spanish
needles, havocking the bees, their bronze staining

my shanks, rain pistils sprung out of the earth and buried
glass splinters under my clothesline. Vivaldi and tangerine

below the early winter moon minting its double
over the city axled down in the buried sea's lilac

silver trimming my window wick with the fierce,
fast and low rustle of lions out of a russeted ice floe.

3

A furnace in my father's voice; I prayed for the coal-stove's
roses, a cruise ship lit like a castle

on fire in the harbour we never walked;
father and son, father drifting down the ferned hell his
    shanty shone, where,

inside, in my head, the lamp was the lamp.
The market, the park, the library not a soul

but grandmother's morning wash lifting towards heaven,
her flapping winding sheets; the barrister sun punished my
    sister, I stared at my hand

in a book, the horizon declined in my mouth, a hawk's
    scream tied all the hills together.
My little earth-shaker, visored in placenta, wonder of

wonders, tremulous in amniotic
shield, ensoulled already, father in the veritable

night, without house or harbour,
soon sea in a voice will harrow

a scorpion's blaze in me, to the marrow.

4

At nights birds hammered my unborn
child's heart, each strike bringing bones

and spine to glow, her lungs pestled
loud as the sea I was raised a sea anemone

among women who cursed their hearts
out, soured themselves, never-brides,

into veranda shades, talcum and tea moistened
their quivering jaws, prophetic without prophecy.

Anvil-black, gleaming garlic nubs, the pageant arrived with
    sails unfurled
from Colchis and I rejoiced like a broken

asylum, to see burning sand grains, skittering ice;
shekels clapped in my chest, I smashed my head against a
    lightbulb

and light sprinkled my hair; I rejoiced, a poui
tree hit by the sun in the room, a man, a man.

5

The sky is loaded with ore, the mountains
the mountains are lingering on the threshold,

luminous with the valley's pollution. A late transport
shimmers, and I shimmer, too: this is one of the holy cities
   of America;

holy banks, mortuaries, holy cafés a golden angel
descends in the middle of three javelining spires.

Then I see poised, wraithlike, in the snow,
on the sifted avenue, muscles released from chiaroscuro,

a herd of darkness gathering to passage unto Shiloh,
where the Lord of Summer lives, kindling a coal fire.

SMALL FANTASIA:
LIGHT YEARS

A soft light, God's idleness
warms the skin of the lake.
Impeachable, thought-changing
light in the mind of the leaves.
What is terrifying about happiness?
Happiness. The water does not move.
God's idleness is everywhere
in the October and November
inlet, where the leaves sleep far
from the married corpses,
bound by a pure, inexplicable love.

THERE

The serial killer line in Chaucer bloomed—
"the smylere with the knyf under the cloke"—
in my head down Bolton Hill, a perfect epitaph

for this city Frederick Douglass's beard braced
through a slight tourist crowd milling at the harbour,
below the bloodshot sign of the Domino Sugar

building, flashing: GHETTOS BEYOND THIS POINT;
there whole blocks shushed by some medieval plague;
there traffic baulked for miles into a blaring cortège;

there a current pulled me one morning after beating
out the fretted equanimity nested on my tender crops,
who winced and sang the *Tales*, for I, triste-tropiques-man,

ice-pick raconteur, who love the spondee of the furnace,
feared a knife sliced my throat, chipped over an imaginary
moat; an anachronistic river sighed below the asphalt,

I heard a man yell in his cell: "Get the fucking money, Pete!";
I lowered my head, holy, as daylight paled into a horse
pluming towards me; I laughed; it halted, "O my chevalier!"

MR. KILLDEER'S
COLD COMFORT

My neighbour, Mr. Killdeer,
crosses with peaches and jalapeños

all through January's silence,
to thaw the hiatus in my ivy

and holly home, a candle
lit at dusk to shadows scrutinizing

from corners, stretching to touch
our low voices on the porch.

Mr. Killdeer, forensic, slices
a peach, pits a pepper, "My wife, Darla,

is a straight shot, great with the M1911 . . ."
and so forth, guttering, until,

heliotropic, green-eyed gristles
stare up from the plate. I raise one

and bite into bone-cold air.
His eyes water, mine for the basalt,

sun-incubating-frosted streets,
the cathedral bells' quarterly

obit phlegms up in my ears.
I do not sleep; I kneel nights

in the book barracks, hoarding
a caravel to return to my birth

sea, back to the tuning-fork peninsula,
an opened valve contradiction

in the town square, the roadside
cane flags glinting through marl

and dust out at Folly Oval,
the cemetery tumbling down

to the barley cricket pitch.
My brain edges: *In this America,*

this wilderness . . . too long dumb,
Mr. Killdeer folds his Swiss,

departs into the snow.
I rise to reenter the Artic

silhouette, certain it is no longer
a miracle to stand on water.

SINGING SCHOOL
VALEDICTION

A scarlet breeze buoyed him next to us,
his white feather hair a boy's, giddy and bright
for this, what he called, "the immaculate air."
It never crossed my mind the wind could be fostered
down to such a casual vision, a taper of crocus
spied through a bubble level. Daily I have
climbed the mound to teach my seminars, some
days I dared look back, pushing the glass door,
at what was reflected in the glass; vermillion
shock of trees, a sky that swims blue and unbroken
with clouds, merging with those brindled hills,
some a wink of gold corona through power lines.
Always I disappeared inside before an eagle fell
from the sun, or whatever was subsequent to sun,
and charged the kids: recite. I listened, distanced.
But now, tuned to his big turnip face, fringed peat
moss sprouts from his ears, blackbird black brows
perked, flicker antennas, pulling from the air
words that filled our small, nervous compass

hearts with the love-harp light he twined between

us, I became a thicket of ears, tensed to engrave,

by instinct, the gradient shifts of his voice

before he scaled the promontory, a kingfisher

hushed back into the chrysalis he sang to us from.

AFTER POMPEII

When the rivers sing in this country
of drunk rivers, the ovens dance;
the city's heart splayed on that cobbled
lane was transplanted from Pompeii,

the Pompeii great rains fell coins
fullones took and spun into silk,
so we who walk in daylight are walking
on the cries of a wild feast;

when we walk the smoke-pummelled
sky, women sizzle like seltzer and bells
striking noon on terraces. The squares
are melting gelatos pageants of tankers

glide to General Sulla's order; war pigeons
drop Morse to submarines buried
under a Medici's robe; an out-of-work
professor, who is also an assassin,

hangs a bag of oranges on a tree
in the park, crosses his legs and sleeps
and dreams an orchard of orange
trees on the Orange Blossom Coast.

The alley shadows are not shy:
tenderness opens in their cool
darkness and under flowering
marquees and in cafés and pizza joints;

tenderness is affordable, and we spend
like nothing, for the day when a breeze
shakes us in twilight, as it shook
the leaves on the villa of the baker

Terentius Neo—but that was no
breeze; a sigh of the first flame
from an oil lamp licking mirrors,
the river, the curtains; strumming

a vase, the hills: Neo's wife in her red
cloak, a rock guitar solo dashing white
bulls into the sea and we, we sink
into the fray of a bright, brass music.

TROUBLE ON
THE ROAD AGAIN

Scavenging down the blue potholed hill, rocking
out of cobalt acid, they steam chromatic, these Elijahs
in their cloud wheels, fatherless and man-killing,
their guts bloated with red heat, lice, cast-iron soldiers
who frighten you into a jacaranda's scattered stare,
making your poor heart rain, everyday trembling

from the exhalation of their shunting furnaces
without backseats, only peril tingling Thy Kingdom
Come, so they come, helicoptering their menace
for the fishing industry, dying, the banana, dead
after so much foreign pesticide maimed the coastline.
They sometimes weep silently passing Arcadia,
but now their coffins beetling crazy music carve down
Free School Hill, rille-shambling and pitching along

into the common light of day, aiming to assault
the town, to circle the bleached clock tower
madmen shade and smoke with mongrels,

and then invade the market, the pier, the square
scorched to a crusty bleb of worries and quarrels.
Here their fleets arrive, closing the circuit, shaking
up dust, diminishing your eyes as they leap
to the waiting pavement, and even beyond that.

SPRAWL

Amid ice and granite
sea hush and crash
and the profit and the loss

the prophet xeroxed
in his tamarind shade
and wasp buzz and saw

in the hills crashed leaves
and virgins' suicides
right after the election

and November's Janus
and Pontius Pilate's
maggot snipers' amen

and fortunately I forgot
to be afraid and kept
my fear in the salt

chiseling my face
when I read Keats
and loved the ash

and put two coins
in my right palm
amid the crashed crop

century of wheat
drought rosary terra
cotta Kali reconnaissance

renaissanced my nipples
torpedoed and rocked
the strobe-lit stageshow

the Gorgon's scintillated
romance foiled the constable's
peace and Herodotus

slept as the prophet rose
to his chalice and put
on his mongrel pelt

and it rained softly
and blessed nothing
scarce of breath

and grated nutmeg
and the tyranny of sugar
and pure cream soda

enclosed in cinders

shook burst fizzed

and I found my shape

shifted ciphered raw

my total reversal

my total reversal

my total reversal

THE ORATOR

Amid a ratcheted, alloyed ghost,
I returned stares in the blackout
that clogged the podium where a bore
was harping in dead metaphor
the horror of colonial heritage.
I sank in the dark, hemorrhaged.
There I remembered the peninsula
of my sea, the breeze opening the water
to no book but dusk; no electricity,
just stars pulsing over shanties,
and, later, an inextinguishable moon,
invisible in this dark NYC room,
a tweeded rodent scholar lectured
on his authority of "Caribbean Culture,"
phosphorus Caliban, switching dialectics
in a single line, praising and cussing metrics:
Rhodesia now, Zimbabwe after;
he real cool, a true, heretical dapper,
but in the surprised blackness,
his soul exposed, the façade recessed,
I saw the face that curried Pelops

in the Antilles to straddle the ivory laps
of liberal, money-giving chaps
with an itch for the unscripted Folk
and Oral Tradition, a hot spoke
in his spinning radius unveiling
the veil of the shroud of the curtain,
and with spectroscopic effect, he has dazzled
all and proven to be ebony solid.
His mouth soured winter, his neck
hung with silk and not a speck
of truth, that I almost shouted, *Please,*
be honest with your lies, disease,
but only stared at this wine-for-rum,
lectern-for-veranda, brilliant scum
who shook when thunder shocked
away Edison's filaments: a dead watt.
Inarticulate at the dark lectern,
he stood grasping what he had learned
in all the colleges, but went hollow
and I heard his breath in shallow
bursts the way a firefly's ticks amplify
a lonely room, each tick signified
his mother back home, who still,
after many years, her only skill,
cleans uptown houses to knuckle

out a living; another tick, his supple,

ever-ready sister, breeding at the first attention

by a name-brand-looker, diamond-

single-earring rude boy, hoping

for foreign, like him in the dark, hiding

behind his varnished gibbet,

he who had stretched out his hand to let

me shake it, smiled, said, "Friend,"

when before he gibbered, "Nemesis; vermin"

to his tail-gawking, maggot rabble.

Confounded, silent in his Babel,

power returned and dragged off

the dark and showed his face caught

in a childhood glare, where the kerosene

shielded flame, the only light to be seen

in his world, enchanted his shadow

on a wall, proof he was two in tow;

jackal and man, duel umbrage,

scavenging years have taken to forge

into one chain; yes, Christ, chain,

he is chatteled within them again.

"Applaud the fluorescence!" he cried.

I couldn't, those bulbs hurt my eyes.

READING LATE: *ANABASIS*

You read the ripples of their sandals
and armours dragged in dust, the anagram
of crows following them, the air,

sick-riveted, pitched down in night's
large territory, near a highway trucks rumbled
like tankers off to war, breath riding

upon water, condensing time—night
the sun's drop into ashes.
You looked up and saw barbarians gathering,

you heard their organs and the stars
when they shouted: Sea! Sea! at the dark
coastline, regiment after regiment, entered.

So you pulled the cord on the light, to wade
the sepia sheets, trouble on the road, forever
the bonfire raging in the skull and bones:

there is nothing strictly immortall, but immortality.

THE NIGHT AUTOBIOGRAPHIES OF LEOPOLD DICE

Not another man to outtalk Leopold Dice;
all when the overproof rum dries up and flies
get brave enough to pitch and sleep on the dominoes,
putting more black eyes into the tiles, and moths
falling in the ice, now pure-so water, dust off
their wings catching gold in the bucket from the bulb
dropped from the ceiling in Coolieman's gambling
shop, Leopold Dice, spirited, measures out stories
all about himself in the peanie wallies' shir-shirring
and the tarpaulin's grunts when a breeze slaps it;
we do our best to look awake, rocking on wooden
stools, leaning on raw posts, the dark outside
and the walk back home in our heads, frightened
of duppy and thief together, and an owl's on-and-off
coarse screech in the manchineel, interfering
but not stopping Leopold Dice, who, in the prime
of another memory, stabs a finger out into the night

to tell us when he was Commissioner of Water—
we know it well—he was the first man to drive
an opened-back Morris up Stony Hill, long before
asphalt; a marine chariot, the piston butter-smooth,
he lights a cigarette, exhales, a better ride Ezekiel
himself couldn't find to heaven; he loved how the Morris
sounded—soundless—when he drove those Sundays
through the bamboo road to Rio Grande, raftsmen
spurring tourists downriver shouted his name
across the water and he honked, the white people
smiled, but hardly two years passed and all the shocks
got loose and the engine started to slog like a battered
dray horse due to potholes and the merciless work
of making water pipes reach every single yard
bush and gully swallowed all over Portland,
the Morris, dead before any of us born, nearly broke
his pocket and spirit with all the trips to Bell Auto
Repairs, but what griped him most, to this day,
after all the miracles he had to perform to plant
the main pump down at Ransa Reservoir,
all in the name of his Party, not a drip came
to the taps, worse it was on the eve of election,
the wrench he used to strike the pump twice
echoed in his hand, the man the Ministry of Water
sent from Kingston, smiling in front of the crowd,

in suit and long rubber boots, stopped smiling

and started looking as if his mother just died,

a look that said *There goes the votes*, the look

that made Leopold Dice give up water, braps so,

for everybody knows, he stresses always at this point,

how ruthless politicians were then—worser than now,

for a hitman, then, was thruppence a piece, so he "fly way"—

a term he grates his teeth on—to Miami, to pick fruits

in the glades, every day wishing he had gone to Panama,

but Lord, everything was in Miami, the only tension

was America mad to drop nuclear on Cuba,

pigs even invaded a beach there, Leopold Dice stubs

his cigarette, but they were bayoneted by the Bloc,

yet the true tension, hotter than nations, was Isabel

Fernández García, herself Cuban, who he was pledging

out his soul-case to, she dredged all the money

he made in those swamps sinuated with mosquitoes

he was so afraid a snake or something wild would turn

him paraplegic; Isabel García, a real black widow,

Leopold Dice sucks his teeth remembering that life,

but concedes, as we expected, squinting, the heartache

she was causing forced him back, dreadlocked, nearly mad,

to his birth rock, now independent of Britain, rum

like leggo-beast in the roads, Leopold Dice laughs,

the owl screeches again, he remembers roaming,

hiccupping with his old water-bird friends, screaming
"GOD BLESSED THE QUEEN AND THE QUEEN'S DRAWERS!",
outwardly he was a lark, though the island was no longer
the green of his Party but orange of the Opposition,
and inside, where it mattered, he couldn't stand
those new aviator-wearing politicians with their orange
badges, orange flags, orange T-shirts, orange motorcades—
orange, the colour of the damn fruits he picked
so many bushels of in Florida, only the sun
left to be pulled down in one of those wicker buckets;
even now rind scent sickens him, anything citrus
does if it is not cut with rum, for rum was life
then, it covered him like a soutane, he draws
an invisible cloth down his body to show us
how it swam over him, always, this time of the night,
his voice slows, from somewhere a stillness
reaches for us, catches us, and we listen for the return,
his voice slower, a croak; his eyes twinkle when he says
the dice rolled his lucky number one night at a Bryans
Bay beach session where he met the local baker, May,
selling her coconut drops, grater cakes, gizzardas,
potato puddings with hallelujah in the middle,
her ginger beer so strong it burned his throat for days,
purged him clean of wonder, rum, and other women,
and yes, he admits grounding his walking stick

he didn't really need, lifts himself up, they're not married,

after thirty-something years under the same roof,

pissing in the same chamber, selling her bake goods

together; even still, Sweet May, whose real husband

not even God can make head or tail of his whereabouts,

was Leopold Dice's wife to the grizzle, May was salvation

ownself after America, he nods, one jaw glossy

in the bulb; then, finally, pocketing his pack

of Craven "A" cigarettes, flaps on his felt, he repeats

the one phrase of true adjournment: Night, night;

walk good until tomorrow again, stepping into

the dark home, we too shuffling up, Coolieman

twisting the bulb off, we hear Leopold Dice shake

the kerosene oil in the soda-bottle torch, strike

a match for the newspaper wick; the flame catches

as we walk out to the dark trees and hills of Port Antonio.

SECOND RETURN

Let the cerement of light, the silent snow
covering the bells frozen in the towers, speak

a country of tired bays, where rain hesitates
to break the seamless yellow of toil; let this

coffin-shaped light balance on the negative
compass, the shock and stun, the heart's

sudden brace for a jealous thunder, childhood's
hands clapping in the assembly of absence,
rejoicing in the clarity of hunger and fired clay.

Let the hands be wings to lift out of water
a rippled name—jangle of bells—left untended,

like a wheat field, swath of light, violet
stains, the night someone wiped her hands

on. Let the stray goat be recalled, and the
mango tree, violated for its bastard fruit, recall

the army of cane flags that marched through
dreams, saluted by silver-edged cutlasses

at morning. O envy of sea, binding and separating
islands, husk envy at every accent's core,

their fiber glint after rum flasks break their seals
and rivers let down their hair between shallow gullies.

Let not the blank of winter forget the buried glass;
let it pull blood out of any pilgrim who goes there

and marks a way back by the body's scent
and light, distended, by a melting brook.

THE SMALL DARK INTERIOR

The child seated in front,
her face close to the glass,
declared the pond frozen.
I was watching the shifting,
bronze grass and strayed
at her verdict. Her father
agreed too, but neatly distilled:
Glossed, honey, a bit iced—
but she was already
onto the drift-pocked, solitary
ducks across the bay's industrial
ruts, their stark white shapes
moving like phantoms in the marsh,
somewhere outside New Jersey.

I followed her pale head's
patient motion towards remnants
of what she saw—quiet now,
left hand at her jaw, the right dimmed

into her father's lap, a deeper silence.
Little Penseuse, I wanted to console:
you see the scene because you think it.
Then, instantly, the silver bullet
entered a tunnel and bound us
in the void, the hiss of steel a sea
straining homeward: *That is the land of lost content . . .*
But the child's reflection wiped
off the glass, and I panicked,
understanding what she meant
at the pond the autumnal
grass did not stir:
Instinct is older than the body.

As my eyes adjusted,
I found her, same position,
in the small dark, and decided
I am ready to forgive
my father his own flawed life.

ACKNOWLEDGMENTS

Grateful acknowledgment is made to the editors of the following
publications, in which some of these poems first appeared,
sometimes in slightly different form: *Blackbox Manifold,
The Buenos Aires Review, Callaloo, Caribbean Review of Books,
The Common, Connotation Press, Foothill Journal, Granta,
Harvard Review, H.O.W. Journal, The Huffington Post,
likestarlings.com, McSweeney's, Memorious Journal, Narrative
Magazine, The Nation, New Issues, The Paris Review, Ploughshares,
Poetry, Poetry International, Poetry Review, Poetry Wales, Prairie
Schooner, Salamander, Small Axe, Urbanite,* and *The Wolf.*